JACK W. HAYFORD

HOPE

WHEN YOU NEED IT MOST

Regal

For more information and
special offers from Regal Books, email us at
subscribe@regalbooks.com

Published by Regal Books
From Gospel Light
Ventura, California, U.S.A.
Printed in the U.S.A.

Originally published as *How to Live Through a Bad Day*, published by
Thomas Nelson, Inc. in 2001.

All personal stories are true. Except for self and family references by
the author, names have been changed to protect confidentiality.

Library of Congress Cataloging-in-Publication Data
Hayford, Jack W.
[How to live through a bad day]
Hope for a hopeless day / Jack W. Hayford.
p. cm.
Originally published: How to live through a bad day. Nashville :
Thomas Nelson, c2001.
ISBN 978-0-8307-4494-7 (trade paper)
ISBN 978-0-8307-7045-8 (special edition)
1. Jesus Christ—Seven last words. 2. Christian life. I. Title.
BT457.H39 2007
232.96'35—dc22
2007021805

Rights for publishing this book in other languages are
contracted by Gospel Light Worldwide, the international nonprofit
ministry of Gospel Light. For additional information, visit
www.gospellightworldwide.org.

CONTENTS

PREFACE

Hopeless days are commonplace in our world.

That isn't a cynical observation. It's an honest one. And in many regards, the same kinds of things that lead to hopeless days for people like you and me were experienced and overcome on one very big day, a long time ago.

This is a small book about that big day. Moreover, it is about an even larger *wonder*—the miracle power in the words spoken on that day, sometimes called the Seven Last Words of Christ, by the One who turned the ultimate bad day into one that history now calls "good." We still call it that today. Every year, when the calendar rolls around at springtime, we arrive there two days before Easter: It's called Good Friday.

There are many reasons Good Friday is called "good," but they are not related to our usual human notions of "nice, happy or comfortable." Rather, the "good" in that day is that it was the day Jesus, who had arrived in Bethlehem years before, surrendered to death on a Cross in Jerusalem.

The "good" is in the Good Shepherd, laying His life down for His sheep.

The "good" is also in the mystery revealed in the fact that, at the price of Jesus' lifeblood, forgiveness for my sin and yours is now a God-given provision offering eternal hope and promise.

Although there are many good reasons why we call *that* Friday "good," it was in reality a very bad day.

It was a day filled with many of the same things that make our days bad at times—bad things that sap the life out of living and wring hope out of our hearts.

It was a day that involved being bitterly betrayed;

It was a day of being beaten brutally—abused hatefully, and of blood and tears;
It was a day of being rejected, of stark loneliness, of friends running away and of enemies dealing violence.

It's the bad day called "Good Friday" because Jesus did things that day that have resulted in an unshakable source of *hope*—hope that saves us, hope that will keep us, hope that will accompany us and hope that will carry us through.

I have written this book because I want to relay something that I learned about hope from Jesus' day of dismal darkness, thunder and earthquake—that "God-forsaken" day in which God Himself was killed as He submitted Himself to the hands of His own creatures. I learned how that day, beyond all others (and yet so much like a thousand of our own in certain ways), holds the keys that open the doorways to hope. And how that bad day in Jesus' life we call good is the reason we will always have hope when we need it most.

Before I share what I have learned from the circumstances of Good Friday and the Seven Last Words Jesus spoke in response, I'm going to bare my soul and tell you about the morning of an awful day in my life, a day of utter hopelessness brought about by circumstance and enunciated by a biting voice that sought to tear hope away. I will share with you, dear reader, how my experience that day prompted me to call on the One Who is able to teach us the words that can turn a hopeless day into a transformed one.

Is it possible for you to find hope when you need it most? Absolutely, and not because of anything you can do, but because of what Jesus has already done.

CHAPTER 1

WHEN IT'S DARK EVERYWHERE AROUND

It was pitch black in the bedroom as I opened my eyes on the morning of October 24, 2003. The digital clock on my bedside table registered precisely five o'clock, a fact confirmed by the chimes I heard from the grandfather clock down the hall in our living room. It had now been 33 hours since Scott had collapsed. It happened instantly—his skull flooded internally with blood as a congenital aneurysm burst and the hemorrhage began to crush his brain stem toward lifelessness. By most evidences he was gone from that moment, though doctors worked valiantly on his behalf, and our church prayed passionately for their pastor.

Scott Bauer, Anna's and my son-in-law, had married our daughter Rebecca over 25 years earlier and had assumed my role as pastor of The Church On The Way, succeeding me after my 30 years as senior pastor there. This decision had not been choreographed by us—neither Scott nor I had ever discussed his following me as pastor, even though his 11 years as my associate would have seemed to suggest it. But our church, while led by the pastor, is governed by godly eldership. Few can imagine my joy when they asked Scott to serve them as God called me away to found The King's Seminary—a new center for training pastoral leaders for the twenty-first century. The church had continued to thrive under the leadership of Scott Bauer—a highly gifted, servant-hearted and Spirit-anointed shepherd of souls. That had suddenly changed 33 hours earlier.

And now, that morning of October 24, 2003— *exactly four years to the day of his being installed as pastor*—at just 49 years of age, the only things keeping Scott's heart functioning were devices scheduled to be "unplugged" at two o'clock that afternoon. Every vestige of sustainable life was gone. Scott, the man who was "my son according to the common faith in Christ," the husband of our oldest child and the father of three of our grandchildren—Scott, the pastor upon whom I, along with the elders of our church, *earlier* had laid hands as he became senior pastor—was gone! The final gesture indicating closure remained until that afternoon, when his parents would arrive from Texas; but in fact, Scott had been declared brain-dead within hours of his collapse.

That had happened Wednesday night. Scott had stepped forward to dismiss the mid-week service, which earlier had been graced by a guest speaker, and then paused for a moment—seemingly bewildered after he had asked the congregation to stand for the benediction. He turned to Dr. Jack Hamilton, one of our pastoral team, and said, "Jack, come and dismiss the service." Then he stepped down the platform stairs in what seemed a natural way, putting his hand to his head as he walked toward his wife who was seated in the front row. But he didn't make it that far. Yet because the congregation was already standing and at prayer, virtually no one saw their beloved pastor as he was assisted—carried from the room by his son, Kyle, and two other men. Though a few minutes later, a brief consciousness was regained, and notwithstanding that almost immediate attention was provided by the paramedics, a precious son and beloved husband and father had lapsed into an unresponsive abyss.

That was the situation to which I awoke at five o'clock that Friday morning. And it wasn't as if we hadn't prayed.

Even though we had been told that Scott's condition was irreversible, prayer had been raised by thousands in the meantime. Still, notwithstanding our hope that a remarkable, unusual dimension of miracle would take place—a miracle which all of us asked and prayed for—the family was at rest that the right decision had been made. Not only had medical evidence verified the propriety of that action, but also the sense we all had that Scott was gone confirmed its wisdom. Still, we never gave up praying. More prayer per square inch than I think I've ever seen went up across the face of this planet on Scott's behalf. We received notices from everywhere, including from the office of President George Bush that our son had been lifted up in prayer at the White House. Hindsight assures us that Scott Bauer did not depart this earth for want of faith or prayer, nor do any of us believe he breathed one breath less than divinely ordained for his earthly sojourn. But *that* confidence came later. Right now it was Friday, and it was dark—very dark—in our bedroom.

The voice that whispered a gravelly snarl was from the Darkness, too.

"So these are the blessings of autumn!!" It was the most vicious, hateful, sinister sound I have ever heard in my life. It was "aloud" in the room, but the whisper to my soul was leveled like a knife—and I knew its source.

It's a risky matter to tell people about occasions when you hear the voice of God, and even more risky if you suggest you heard the voice of

Satan. But I have never been mystical nor given to a quest for such experiences. Still, on a few occasions when I felt it might help people understand God's Word of truth and the realities of life, I have related such things from my own lifelong walk with Christ, which has been a Bible-centered, Spirit-filled life of faith.

The hate-filled, heinous words—threaded with an icy fury—require explanation, for they were spoken as a despicable mockery, spewing back at me a statement I had testified to Father God's having spoken to me several years earlier. Now I was age 68, but nearly a decade before, our loving God had clearly impressed me that the autumn years of my life would be filled with and attended by profound promise and hope. From that time, at so many points, those promises had been and were continuing to be verified, notwithstanding this shocking, present moment. But now, in the darkness of this Friday morning, Satan himself was seeking to capitalize on our trial and spit in the face of the gracious "future hope" that God had declared to be His will for me: "I will give you the blessings of autumn."

As anyone who's ever heard me speak about it knows, autumn is my favorite season of the year. It holds the ingathering of the harvest. It holds the greatest celebrations. And it unfolds such breathtaking beauty in the blaze of its colorful splendor.

But now, in the early morning darkness of that dreadful autumnal Friday in October, facing both the certainty of what was ahead for Scott, as well as the uncertainty of what was ahead for me, I heard that brutal, hateful voice. The prince of hell issued forth a taunting, sinister laugh, adding, "Everything will collapse along with Scott. The church will not withstand this shock, the seminary vision will falter and fail, and the faith of those who have prayed will turn to futility and abiding doubt!"

In the first instant of that encounter—confronted by the presence of the Evil One, encompassed by the darkness of the hour and facing the painful reality of Scott's situation—the moment was nearly as absolutely crushing as any I've ever known.

I think you, dear reader, know precisely what I'm talking about here. Honest hearts who have faced, or who are facing, a dark trial will admit to experiencing moments when God's promises are so brutally challenged by the Liar, and when the darkness of the hour argues that all hope is a lie—that hopelessness seems about to win. But besides being honest, our hearts need to learn to be *wise* at such moments. By God's grace, I had faced that Liar enough times to know what to do.

Exhausted and unable to even attempt a rebuttal or to strike a bold stance against so merciless and penetratingly personal an assault, I simply turned back over in bed. Rolling onto my side, I quietly lifted my voice to another One, saying, "Jesus, You are going to have to handle this." That was all I said—and it was all I needed.

Just like that, as though a hand passed over my face and closed my eyes, I fell back asleep—a phenomenon completely unlike me when I awake in the morning, for when I wake up, *I'm awake* for the day. But I don't even remember closing my eyes—it was just as if the Savior *took it all away*. I awoke exactly one hour later and opened my eyes to see the digital display, six o'clock, and then, as before, I heard the chimes from the front of the house. However, upon this waking, two things were very different.

First, the morning light had begun to illuminate the room with a slight but welcomed grayness. Second, as I rose and sat on the edge of my bed, an indescribable miracle had taken place.

I was enveloped with an overwhelming sense of the PEACE OF GOD!

I use all capital letters because I know of no other way to describe how, for the first time in my life, I believe I truly experienced "the peace of God, which surpasses all understanding" (Phil. 4:7).

When I stood up, it was as though I had stepped onto a block of granite a mile in each direction. I felt an unshakable sense of being totally, mightily and majestically undergirded by the power of God in a manner that transcended any security, confidence or peace I'd ever experienced.

From there, I stepped into that Friday—and on into the weekend, and then the weeks and months that followed. Each had their challenges. I was asked to return to the church as pastor for a year until a new pastor could be positioned. That call not only compounded my duties, but it also meant I would need to lead that dear flock through the immediate challenge of grieving the death of their pastor, while navigating Anna's and my grief, along with that of our daughter and her family, as well as the rest of our family.

But something happened that Friday that unleashed the power of another Friday.

It was the Friday that Jesus paid it all, suffered it all, died for all, and *won it all!* And it is at the heart of my writing this book to *you*, dear child of God.

The peace and the eventual victory-beyond-hopelessness that I gained were through no achievement of my great faith. When you're down on your back, when everything of your circumstance is surrounded by darkness, and when the voice seeking to capture your attention sneers against

God and seeks to smash your soul with despair—it's at those moments we're called to remember another Voice. It's the voice of Jesus, calling us from the other side of His Cross, where He experienced everything that pain, suffering, hopelessness, hate, death and hell could deal Him. And He's saying, "Call on Me—I know the way through Fridays like yours, and I will bring you through!"

There is hope—for any and every hopeless day. We each need not only to listen to His call but also to understand the pathway He has carved beyond hopelessness and unto hope. So I invite you to join me in listening to His voice as Jesus lives through a bad day—indeed, not only through the worst day in His life, but also the ultimate worst day that humans or demons could ever conspire to work.

There's hope here. I know because I've experienced it often—including on the worst day I've ever known. And on such days, it awaits each of us to discover for ourselves the timeless promise:

> *The eternal God is your refuge, and underneath are the everlasting arms.*
>
> DEUTERONOMY 33:27

CHAPTER 2

FINDING HOPE IN A HOPELESS DAY

*Let us run with endurance the race that is set before us,
looking unto Jesus, the author and finisher of our faith,
who for the joy that was set before Him endured the cross.*

HEBREWS 12:1-2

The morning I have just described turned a *hopeless* day around—took the *"less"* out of that word, and left the remaining gift to me of an authentic, deep-seated, dynamically sustaining sense of *hope*. The reason for such a solid turnaround and genuine infusion of hope is explainable. It's wrapped up in the three words that are found in the text above: *"looking unto Jesus."* In short, "hope" is derived from the direction we look. If we look at circumstances, at ourselves, at the past or at trends—if we look at the situation from any other view than through the lens of faith—we get *less*. Turning our eyes instead toward God's redemptive, recovering, restoring possibilities, which are always available through His Son, is the pivot point. Turning to *Him* is the turning point: *"looking unto Jesus!"*

That directive, when your hope level is down to low or nothing, isn't a religious summons; it's a signpost toward a pathway that will provide two things: a Director and a destination. The first, of course, is the Savior—the Man like no other, because He is God above all—Jesus, who suffered the horrors of a Friday because He was en route to the hope- and joy-filled reality of a Sunday.

His Friday was a pathway toward the Resurrection, even if all we can see on that day is apparent agony and depressing defeat that appears to end with His body being placed in a hopeless hole in the ground. But a succession of statements constitute the trail He blazed as the pioneer—the author, initiator and founder—of our faith. To listen to Him speak from His Cross on that Friday is to learn to walk toward hope when we face our hopeless days.

So come with me as we measure the meaning and consider the counsel of this One Who says, "Take up [your] cross and follow Me" (Mark 8:34). Since His purpose in life was that you and I might have "life, and life abundantly," and His provision in death was to "save all that are lost and . . . to destroy the works of the devil," we can count on this: His Cross is the pathway to hope.

Hopeless days happen in the lives of everyone. They come more often than we think we deserve, and they sometimes last much longer than we think we can stand. That's the reason every disciple of Jesus needs to have a framework for processing hopeless days. And God's Word directs us to one: "Let us run with endurance the race that is set before us, looking unto Jesus, the author and finisher of our faith, who for the joy that was set before Him endured the cross" (Heb. 12:1-2).

When I see people experience one of life's hopeless days, I've learned to urge them to come again to the Cross. That invitation is *not* to commiserate over the agonies suffered there, as though Jesus may take comfort in our feeling bad all over again about what happened there. He calls us to the Cross to find *life*—first, through receiving the forgiveness God offers each of us through His Son. And then He calls us to *learn to live*—to find companionship and power-filled guidance from Him when you and I face our "cross" days.

The sum of human pain, problem, futility and hopelessness is focused here at the Cross of Christ—*all* suffering, *all* rejection, *all* painfulness,
> *all* exhaustion, *all* misunderstanding,
> *all* anger, *all* hatred, *all* sinning, *all* depression,
> *all* loneliness, *all* death.

But also focused here is *all* wisdom and understanding,
> and *all* faith, hope and love.

It is by and unto that love we are summoned most of all—to look unto Jesus and to welcome Him into our hopeless days, having seen Him process what may well have been His . . . *except*. The exception is that Jesus handled the day in a way that saw beyond it: "For the joy that was set before Him, [He] endured the Cross." He related to each moment and each person in a manner that overthrew their hope-emptying potential, showing us the way to do likewise in any such day we may face.

* * *

The promise was to a band of exiles being led by their captors from the ruins of their ransacked city, Jerusalem. It's another example of God meeting us with case studies in His ways of providing hope. As stumbling, shamed platoons of defeated citizens were being led out of Jerusalem, en route to Babylon at the sword-point of their enemies, Jeremiah raised his voice against the futility they sensed and the presumption they were destined to pointlessness. In God's Name, the prophet declared:

> For I know the thoughts that I think toward you, says the Lord, thoughts of peace and not of evil, to give you a future and a hope. Then you will call upon Me

and go and pray to Me, and I will listen to you. And you will seek Me and find Me, when you search for Me with all your heart. I will be found by you, says the Lord, and I will bring you back from your captivity (Jer. 29:11-14).

The record of history is that God made good on that promise, exactly as He assured those people He would on that discouraging, hopeless day. And that record isn't there to merely *memorize* as a historic fact. It's given to us to *contemporize*—to apply to our present moment as a prophetic promise! We are called to hope just as surely as we are called to the Cross, for the Savior Who speaks there is teaching us the way to live, just as surely as He is dying to give us life.

Come.

Listen to Him relate seven keys that will keep hope's doorway open.

Let me tell you seven stories of people who received His keys *today* and unshackled that which seemed hopeless from their lives—men and women who went free with hope.

Jesus is speaking still. His Cross is a victory now achieved, and the words He spoke there are ready to be applied, to assist you toward achieving your victory as well.

CHAPTER 3

FORGIVE EVERYONE WHO'S TRYING TO RUIN YOUR LIFE

"Father, forgive them for they do not know what they do."

LUKE 23:34

A marvel and a majesty are evident in these first words of Jesus. The blood of the Lamb has just begun to be spilled from the altar of the Cross. The plan for this moment's provision has moved from Eden's first sacrifice for sin and through centuries of multitudinous animal sacrifices, as worshipers were being taught of a Final Sacrifice to come.

Now He is on the Cross—the Lamb of God who takes away the sin of the world.

And now He is presenting Himself—the Great High Priest offering His own life for humankind's greatest need: forgiveness for sin and release from its bondage.

The first words of this Lamb-Priest are *tender* in the face of His hate-filled antagonists, and they are *timeless* and love-filled as they reach to you and me today. But they are also *teaching* words for us who would be taught how to find hope for a hopeless day, and our first lesson is this:

> *To find hope for a hopeless day, begin by forgiving everyone who seems to be trying to ruin your life.*

Hopelessness is as common an emotion and as real a reality as any of us experience. Hopeless days are the result of *things that happen*, and things that happen are the result of things people do.

People who misunderstood.

People who intended to hurt us.

People who forgot or neglected to do something.

People who betrayed or violated us.

People who injured us yesterday . . . or yester*year*.

People *do* things, and what is hardest for us to believe is what Jesus said that day about them: People don't really know what they are doing.

Those words of Jesus—". . . they don't know what they're doing"—are probably the most descriptive truth there is about all human sinning and failure, about our lovelessness, rebellion, hurt, hatred, anger, violence, and the thousand other evils that have overtaken our fallen race. Even when sin is calculated, planned thoroughly, conceived carefully, and executed efficiently, no one really understands the depth or dimension of sin's destructiveness or the degree of its horrible damage to people. In a very real sense, *every* sin is a sin of ignorance.

To learn the grace of forgiveness—to embrace the will to forgive anyone or everyone who seems to be ruining your life right now—a starting place needs to be found, and Jesus points us to it: "They don't know what they're doing."

The fact is, however, that isn't the way we feel. We tend to see things from the viewpoint of *our* experience, and when bad things happen, it looks like whoever did us wrong knew exactly what they were doing—and didn't seem to care, either.

It must have looked that way from the Cross, but Jesus teaches us something about the secret of forgiveness: *Forgiving those who assail you is the key to not being permanently victimized by them.* Whatever the initial impact of any offense done to us by others, our refusal to react, to carry a grudge or to retaliate in-kind secures the high ground. But that must be as real on our part as the Savior's forgiveness, not merely a humanistic, self-willed exercise in self-control. The latter may appear noble, but it only breeds an internalized pride.

True forgiveness springs from gratitude to God for His forgiving me. True forgiveness is born of my remembrance that I have been forgiven so great a debt through God's love that there is no justification for my being less than fully forgiving to others. Because I have "freely received," my Lord calls me to "freely give." To forgive those seeking to injure you or me is to *remove ourselves from their control* and to be unfettered by the anger, pain or disappointment that would seek to attach itself to us.

As I think of the holy reversal that can be brought about by a genuine spirit of forgiveness, Richard comes to mind as a marvelous example of such grace. He disallowed the hopeless day of rejection by a whole circle of friends—one especially—to dominate his heart, and as a result, Richard realized the hope and joy of both a "new day" for himself and a "happy day" of salvation for another. I heard his story firsthand when he visited my office one day.

It had been nearly two years since Richard had come to Christ. His transformation by the power of the gospel and his rediscovery of the Creator's true design for him as a person—as a *man*—had produced a true disciple of Jesus. The pathway out of his former lifestyle of living in the West Hollywood community with his male lover had been more than an experimental excursion. As a professional in the medical community, he was respected for his skills; as a member of the homo-sexual community, he was accepted by a broad circle of like-minded friends. He was the consummate example of all that *any* community would want to designate as a case study for its effectiveness: "He's a success, and he's one of us!"

But it all changed rapidly, almost viciously, when Richard received Jesus as his Savior. The rejection he experienced had nothing to do with reasons a critic might presume: He became neither a self-righteous judge of his friends nor a preachy saint. But he had explained his decision for Christ to his lover, making every effort to assuage wounded emotions when he also announced that he would be discontinuing their relationship. "I care about you, Charles," he said, "but honesty with the truth and faithfulness to the love of God for both of us will not allow me to live as I have anymore. I don't want you to feel I hate you or think you are an unworthy person. I simply know God has a better way for both of us."

The reaction was explosive.

Charles was infuriated and immediately spread the word that Richard had more than simply "done him wrong"; he had become one of "them." In the view of hosts of gays, "them" represents those in the Christian community who appear to devalue the humanity of anyone embracing homosexuality. Many do not resent the Christian's faith as much as they resent what they see in many Christians as being a loathing, demeaning view of them as people. The epithet *abomination* is perceived as a hate-filled, sneering, condescending announcement laced with a social intolerance of individual human rights—motivated by a quest for political control that would exterminate them if Christians ever gained governing power.

And Richard had become one of "them."

Richard's regret was not rooted in either the speed with which his many friends turned their backs on him or in the bitterness that virtually spit at his new life of commitment to Christ. Rather he was broken-hearted over the twisted perception his former friends had of what knowing Jesus is really about, and he was equally regretful for the few cases of supposed "Christian" activity which justified the caricature they drew of "them." And that was what had brought about our meeting at my office that day.

Richard had written me a letter of warm encouragement. He described his having found our church after his conversion to the Savior, and he expressed his deep gratitude for the haven of hope it provided and for the atmosphere for growth he had found. He wrote:

Pastor Jack, it hasn't been easy to find a fellowship which offers both grace and truth. I wanted to say how thankful I am for a congregation that is constant in both: (1) a commitment to God's Word and its requirements for living in God's will (including the call away from sexual disobedience); and (2) a commitment to God's love and its requirements for showing God's grace to the lost (including a generosity of spirit to all who live in a blindness to their sin— seeking to "love them to life" rather than viewing them with condescension).

I was more heart-warmed by his discerning, solidly discipled understanding than I was by his nice remarks about our church. He was a marvelous case of the way that *Jesus saves*. Those two words that summarize the gospel were in full evidence in this man who had been completely transformed—resurrected from a deadly environment and now walking steadfastly in the light of God's Word. Richard was a man who was compassionately concerned about those whom he might reach for Christ, especially those caught in the grip of his own former confusion. Such reasons were heartwarming enough, but I was about to discover something even more profoundly heart-stirring.

Our conversation was concluding when Richard made a request. "Before I go, Pastor Jack, would you mind praying with me about something that's happening right now?" I nodded my head, inviting him to go on. "I want to ask your prayer support for the next few days. Let me explain."

He proceeded to outline briefly how, only a few weeks before, he had received word that his former lover was dying—now under the siege of a virulent assault of AIDS. Hearing that Charles had virtually disappeared from the scene, Richard went to the apartment they had formerly occupied together and found him there. "I knocked on the door, not only wondering if he was there at all, but also feeling very uncertain of what kind of reception I would find if he was," Richard continued.

"When the door cracked open, I was stunned. Charles' face was shriveled; he had open sores; he looked like walking death. As he peered at me through squinting eyes, his face turned to a scowl. He seemed uncertain about opening the door and weakly said, 'Oh, it's you.'"

Richard went on, explaining how Charles had then turned away from the door but had left it open. "If I didn't have the medical training I do, it would have been dangerous to go in, but I did."

The apartment was in disarray and the stuffiness of the room unpleasant with the smell of death encroaching upon a human body. Richard said nothing, but went about cleaning the place as Charles returned to his bed. With the caution and skill of a professional, Richard proceeded to attend to Charles' needs—helping him bathe, cleansing the sores, remaking his bed, and then preparing a dinnertime meal for him.

"There were few words exchanged. Charles was so desperately in need, he could hardly protest the help I was offering, and when I finished washing the dishes I told him I would be back the next day. Pastor Jack, that was nearly four weeks ago, but my request for prayer is because of what happened this week."

I was already near tears as I listened. The manifest purity of Richard's motives, the gracious compassion in his actions, the clear-eyed concern in his words to me—all were the essence of such a Christlike forgivingness. Here he was, reaching where he had been rejected, loving in the most practical of terms and with the purest of objectives.

"In all these weeks of ministering help to him, Pastor, I intentionally did not mention Jesus to Charles, not even once—not because I am ashamed of Him, but because I knew whatever I said wouldn't be received. And then, just three days ago, as I was helping Charles back to bed after changing the sheets, he said, almost with pitiful resignation, 'Okay, Richard. Tell me about Jesus.'"

Both Richard's eyes and my own were misted as he described Charles' opening his heart to the Savior. And I was overcome with this evidence of the power of forgiveness when it is shown toward the very person who has rejected you.

The request was direct: that we pray for Charles' last days on this earth. Neither Richard nor I was devoid of the belief that Christ can heal, at times even in the most extreme circumstances. And neither of us doubted the possibility of willingness within the mercy of God for one whose condition was as the result of so clear a violation of His benevolent intent for humankind. But there was a sense of closure—one that Charles had expressed, and one to which Richard bore witness—that the physically tormented body about to be left behind was no longer the definition of Charles' future. He had received the Savior. He was ready to go. So, we prayed. Two weeks later, another redeemed soul entered eternal glory, and Richard phoned me to report Charles' homegoing.

The most remarkable thing about that story is the evidence it holds of the sheer power inherent in a disciple's learning the Master's overwhelming, unlimited grace of forgiveness. It is not in denying the hopeless days that take place when others reject us or turn on us. It is not in minimizing the pain we experience at the hands of those who seem bent on ruining our lives. People turn on people. They betray one another. Crass unkindness, vicious plottings, horrible and intentional antagonisms are shown, and calling it a hopeless day hardly describes the extended season of struggle that many of us face at times. But there is a lesson at Calvary.

Forgive everyone—anyone—whom you think has failed you, hurt you, offended you. If you think they've done anything to ruin your day, ruin your life, ruin your opportunities, ruin your dreams, or block your goals—*forgive them*. Forgiving others is the key to living in the liberty of the freeing forgiveness Jesus has given us, and it's the first step toward finding hope when you need it most, not to mention opening the door to new days unimagined.

* * *

Is there any fact of your past that you feel traps you? Have you placed it before the Lord, to receive either forgiveness for any failure or deliverance from any bondage you invited by your actions? Hopelessness is untangled and moved to *hope* when we are able to stand before the Father in the full consciousness of a surrendered heart, freed of residual condemnation that He is ready to remove. Read Romans 8.

CHAPTER 4

HELP OTHERS WHO ARE EXPERIENCING YOUR SAME STRUGGLE

"Assuredly, I say to you, today you will be with Me in Paradise."

LUKE 23:43

Exactly how soon the verbal exchange took place isn't clear, but Jesus—suspended on a cross between a pair of thieves also being crucified—was made the subject of a brief debate between them. Luke's report reads:

> Then one of the criminals who were hanged blasphemed Him, saying, "If You are the Christ, save Yourself and us." But the other, answering, rebuked him, saying, "Do you not even fear God, seeing you are under the same condemnation? And we indeed justly, for we receive the due reward of our deeds; but this Man has done nothing

wrong." Then he said to Jesus, "Lord, remember me when You come into Your kingdom." And Jesus said to him, "Assuredly,
I say to you, today you will be with Me in
Paradise" (Luke 23:39-43).

At the beginning of their interchange, Jesus
was only an observer-listener. He was on the
Cross, but there were two others on crosses, one
to His right and one to His left. They were crimi-
nals and, in an apparent coincidence of sched-
uling within the Roman program of execution,
Jesus' hopeless day happens to be their day of
destruction as well. Both men seemed to be aware
of the claims that have been made about Jesus
and knew why He was there. But only one dis-
played cynicism and anger, swearing at Jesus and
making a mocking reference to His power. The
other criminal briskly challenged his counter-
part: "Don't you have any respect? This Man
doesn't deserve that kind of cynicism or bitterness. He hasn't done anything wrong, but we're
getting what we deserve." It was a clear confession
of his own sinfulness. Then, in the same repentant
spirit, and with a distinct and humble acknowledgment of Jesus' divinity, he made a request of
the Savior: "Lord, remember me when You come
into Your kingdom."

Jesus' response is a study in divine mercy, in grace's readiness to give salvation, in God's immeasurable gentleness toward all who come to Him, and in the truth that it is never too late to seek God. It is a scenario that jangles the nerves of the religionist who would haltingly dispense salvation. It is as dramatic a statement God's Son could make to say, "Those who come to Me, I'll never turn away." That's the gospel truth wrapped in this event, but there's a discipling principle as well. In Jesus' response to this hopeless-day encounter, we're taught a second lesson about how to live through such days of our own: Encourage others who are struggling or uncertain.

There are two noteworthy things about Jesus' interaction with the repentant thief. First, the man was experiencing *exactly the same thing* Jesus was. Please capture that. Jesus could have been focused on His own problems, but He demonstrated sensitivity that remained available to the needs of other people around him, even when dealing with His own pain. And in this action, there was something more.

Second, Jesus might have taken a stance as the man's superior, but He readily responded as One engaged in the same hopeless struggle. True, the thief was facing that day with infinitely less resources that Jesus had. Jesus was suffering, but He was—and is—the Lord; even the thief recognized that. Jesus had been pierced at hands and feet with nails, and tortured with a thorn-crown crushed into His head, but He was and is God's King. Yet it was neither from His spiritually royal role nor from a morally superior role that the Savior related to this one who was seeking succor for his soul. He met the man on the common plane of their suffering together on that hopeless day.

Jesus charted the way for our learning that, whatever our hopeless day may involve, He's calling us to meet fellow strugglers where *they* are, refusing to distance ourselves by reason of whatever position or resources we may have. Within God's grace, it's a lesson I have slowly learned. And on one occasion, I was literally shaken up as God exposed me to horrifying fear in order to help me learn that lesson.

Ten thousand freight trains seemed to be thundering through our house at the moment Los Angeles was so violently devastated. It was 4:31, Monday morning, January 17, 1994, when the Northridge earthquake exploded life at a dimension resulting in one of the most cataclysmic natural disasters in American history. Structures as architecturally sound as freeways and multi-storied buildings collapsed like a child's play village. Water mains and gas lines burst, and streets were filled with fire.

My personal experience is unforgettable in a number of ways, but none more awkward than in the emotional trauma I found myself carrying during the days that immediately followed.

It was embarrassing.

Here I was, a man of faith, solidly established in the spiritual resources of God's Word and charged with the leadership of a flock in need of my strength and ministry to encourage them during the aftermath of the disaster—and I was terrified myself. Every jolting aftershock jarred the raw sensitivities of us all, but I doubt that anyone was more traumatized than I was.

It wasn't that I had been injured or suffered a staggering loss such as those whose businesses had been left in shambles or those who had been hurt in the quake. Nor was I among the scores left bereaved by the loss of loved ones killed in related incidents to the massive upheaval. Our family was safe, our home virtually untouched beyond some broken furniture, scattered like toys across the rooms of our house. Still, as night fell on each successive day, I seemed to become another person.

I didn't want to admit to myself, much less to my wife or others, how the inner turmoil seemed to dominate me. It was not quite paralyzing, but it radically inhibited my normal feelings and responses. A trip alone to the other end of the house, especially after dark, nearly terrorized me. Though accustomed to rising in the night to spend an hour or more at prayer in the darkness while the rest of my family slept, after the quake I ventured only to the bathroom in the dark with a flashlight in hand, and even then I was gripped by a sense of fear I had never known.

After four days of those uncharacteristic feelings, I desperately sought God in prayer. I was not frantic, and I was not stampeded by panic, but I was very, very bewildered. "Lord," I exclaimed, "I can't understand myself! I am *not* afraid for my life, and I am *not* in doubt of Your presence and protection. Please help me, Lord. I need Your help. Is something wrong with me?"

Instantly, and with utmost surprise at the immediacy of the response, I sensed an inner whisper to my soul: *"My son, there is nothing wrong with you. I allowed you to experience the depth of the trauma and fear that has gripped multitudes in order that you might understand their torment and comfort them beyond their fears."*

I knew that Voice, and I was immediately drawn to His Word: "Blessed be the God and Father of our Lord Jesus Christ, the Father of mercies and God of all comfort, who comforts us in all our tribulation, that we may be able to comfort those who are in any trouble, with the comfort with which we ourselves are comforted by God" (2 Cor. 1:3-4). It relates one of the classic strategies of the Most High, who uses His children who have endured difficulty to become a strength to others experiencing the same trial. It is the divine reminder that *we comfort others not from the foundation of our superior faith but from the commonality of our mutual struggles.*

The following week I brought one of the most hopeful sermons of my 40 years of pastoral preaching, "Discerning and Dealing with Fears," teaching from 1 John 4:17-19. Not only was my teaching rooted in God's unshakable Word of promise, but I also illustrated it with full, personal transparency—relating my own wrestlings with fear over the preceding days. I risked seeming to be less than a pillar of strength as I opened my heart to vulnerably admit bewilderment with my apparently less-than-faith-filled nights of uneasiness. When I shared the completely unnerving sense of helplessness I'd felt with every aftershock, the people were *strengthened*! Hearts took hope. Eyes began to shine again. Faith was evoked in the wake of my confessing my fears. It seemed paradoxical, but it was the fulfillment of God's own Word—the one source where hope can be found when hopeless days surround you.

The elders of our church agreed to provide for thousands of audiocassette copies of my message to be duplicated and distributed freely via our congregation. Hundreds of people used them to answer their own inner struggle, while hundreds more passed them on to friends and relatives who were experiencing post-quake trauma. The impact was dramatic. And the reason was basically because one lone disciple, tormented by fear where others might have thought him above such distress, was given grace to live out a little of the greatness seen in our Great Savior.

That grace is seen most grandly in the midst of that initial Good Friday—the one hopeless day beyond all hopeless days. As the Son of God assures another fellow sufferer in the middle of His own agony, He not only comforts him with the promise of eternal hope, but He also meets him in the "today" of his struggle with divine promise, the ultimate assurance of hope: "Assuredly . . . today!" Those words were spoken as a *gift* by One whose own struggle did not prevent Him from making Himself available to help others who were also struggling.

It's a prompter we would do well to remember whenever tough days strike, seeking to drive our focus so deeply into our own challenges that we lose perspective on those around us.

Look for the likelihood that in your own hopeless day you might become an instrument to encourage hope in others. To do so isn't to pretend your own struggle isn't real. It's to refuse to allow your heart to be shrunken, just when God is wanting to stretch it to trust Him. Open your heart to reach to others and you'll find yourself receiving hope, even as you are giving it to someone else.

* * *

Have you ever felt called to go beyond your own immediate trial and help someone else through theirs? What did you gain by doing that? What did you lose? The flow of God's grace to us increases as we open to become instruments of His love and hope to others. Read Philippians 2.

CHAPTER 5

BE SURE YOU'VE TAKEN CARE OF THOSE NEAR YOU

"Woman, behold your son . . . Behold your mother!"
JOHN 19:26-27

The third key for discovering hope when you need it most: *Be sure you've taken care of those near you.* Its wisdom flows from the motive and moment of these gentle directives. From the Cross, Jesus first addresses Mary, His mother. Then He speaks to John, the only one of His 12 disciples who followed Jesus all the way to the Cross.

John is the only one of the 12 remaining. The others, for various reasons, have all fled—mostly out of fear. But John stayed with Him—first following Jesus to the place of His trial and then to the scene of His crucifixion. There were also three women at the Cross, probably having joined John earlier in the day at his request. Most notably, considering the pathos of the moment, one of them was Jesus' mother, and the two other women were probably there to attend to her. To watch one's child tortured unto death would be heavy fare for anyone, and supportive friends were needed.

Mary is an interesting study throughout the life of Jesus. She became a disciple of her own son. It's unfortunate that there has been distortion about her role, because Mary herself was never confused about it. From the beginning, she knew the difference between who *she* was and Who *He* was. And when we read of her presence at His death—a brave and noble act, to say the least— we would be blinded by bigotry or devoid of human sensitivity if we did not sympathize with this mother's heartache as she watches her son bear the agony and the torment of His Cross.

That is all very meaningful and quite emotional when we think about it from Mary's side— feeling with her as her maternal instincts were being ripped to shreds. But another matter is present here as well. It was probably not dominant in Mary's mind, but inevitably it was an issue she would have to face sooner rather than later. Mary, the mother of Jesus, must have wondered, "When He's gone, what is going to happen to me?"

Because Jesus was her oldest child, Mary had been essentially subordinate to and dependent upon His care, probably for years. Most scholars suggest that Joseph was much older than Mary and that following his death, Jesus had taken up the management of his business as well as responsibility for leading the family. So now, on the brink of death, is the One who would have been her protector, her "covering" as we often say, especially in a society where women were so frequently disenfranchised by the deaths of the men in their lives. Thus, however noble Mary's maternal concern, she must have also had concern about her future. And again, this Man—God in our midst, Jesus—teaches us more about hope for a hopeless day.

Though He was Himself surrounded by turmoil and the swirling of events targeting His destruction, Jesus turned His concern to His mother's personal plight. When He said, "Woman, behold your son," He wasn't saying, "Look at Me and weep, Mother." He was directing her attention to John. He was saying, "Woman [a term of respect, approximately equivalent to "ma'am"], this man will become the one to oversee you." And completing the transfer of responsibility for His mother, He said to John, "Son, behold your mother."

Let the simple beauty of it speak for itself: Jesus was not assigning a worship relationship from John toward Mary; He was assigning a domestic responsibility. Jesus was committing the care of His mother to the disciple closest to Him, a responsibility that history records John was faithful to accept and fulfill. And in making that assignment, Jesus speaks to each of us in the hopeless days of our own lives to refuse to allow our present pain to dull our sensitivity to the needs of others who depend on us. It demonstrates a magnificence I saw beautifully lived out by Vic after Cora died.

It had happened without warning on a Tuesday morning. Vic's bride of more than a half-century, his partner through a lifetime of service to Christ as a pair of beloved and trusted leaders, was suddenly gone. A heart attack had taken her as she was ushered into eternal glory, and Vic was left, a bereaved husband.

He was never a whimperer—no, not on any terms. No one ever heard a word of complaint during those days following Cora's departure. In fact, Vic's own failing physical condition, accompanied by the grief we all knew was cutting to the center of the soul of a man whose relationship with his wife was as near and dear as anyone could ever imagine, prompted most of us to suppose the obvious: "He'll follow her very, very soon."

Many of us have seen cases where lifelong closeness seems to have uniquely bonded a couple, and where physical weakness or sickness, joined to

JESUS SPEAKS TO EACH
OF US IN THE HOPELESS
DAYS OF OUR OWN LIVES
TO REFUSE TO ALLOW
OUR PRESENT PAIN TO
DULL OUR SENSITIVITY
TO THE NEEDS OF OTHERS
WHO ARE NEAR TO US.

advanced years, puts life's conclusion within antic-
ipatable nearness. When one is gone, the other so
often follows quickly.

We expected this with Vic; though not a welcomed thought, it was nonetheless a reasonable
one—their closeness, his grieving, his physical
decline. *It will be soon*, most friends and family
thought.

But Vic didn't follow at once.

I was a close friend to Vic and Cora and their
children, as well as honored to be called his pastor
during the last decades of his life, so I went to
spend time with him one day. The conversation
was extended, without hurry and certainly without suggesting what many of us thought—that he
would not survive long. But that day I encountered
a man who was praying and willing to live "until
I have a number of things settled." He was very
businesslike and candid about it, acknowledging
something on the order of the apostle Paul's words:
"I am hard-pressed between the two, having a
desire to depart and be with Christ, which is far
better. Nevertheless to remain in the flesh is more
needful for you" (Phil. 1:23-24).

There was nothing of arrogance or humanistic tenacity in his voice or in the stance of Vic's
soul. His intent to pursue life was not a quest for
emotional survival or a self-asserted will to live,

as though he either desperately sought life or felt it was right to commandeer his destiny. Humanly, he would have preferred "going home to heaven," but something else was much on his mind and fixed in his soul. I was deeply touched with a sense of paternal care, personal accountability, and spiritual passion in his whole demeanor.

During the following months, I stayed in touch with Vic. I seldom saw him, but heard from family: Vic was taking care of settling business matters, spending time with grandchildren, engaging in significant conversations with his children, phoning the few of his lifelong friends who were still alive, most of whom were in their eighth and ninth decades of life. And it was almost exactly nine months after Cora died that Vic's daughter called, suggesting I come to see him. "I think he's decided he's finished taking care of things, Jack," she said. And that's just about the same thing he said to me when we talked that last time.

Those nine months, like a pregnancy waiting to bring forth life, were completed, and Vic died. He had always been a man who cared and was concerned for people. Those characteristics made him such a great spiritual leader. And at life's end, when the hopeless day of Cora's departure might have inclined him to simply surrender, he became a man with a yet-unfulfilled mission. In the pattern of his Savior who still kept focus on the need of those around Him while yet nailed to the ultimate hopeless day, Vic focused on life rather than on his grief. He resolved issues concerning others near to him before he let go of life, before going to meet His Lord and to experience heaven's reunion with loved ones already gone ahead. In short, he did not let the difficult days of his grieving turn him into a man without hope or interfere with his attendance to concerns regarding others who would be left behind.

Our Lord's discipling model speaks from this "word" spoken at Calvary: "Son . . . Mother." And it says to you and me: When you're going through a bad day, don't neglect taking care of those who are near to you, for you may yet be the one who brings them hope. We all have a tendency to presume that those closest to us understand our dilemma, and that somehow they will automatically absorb it along with us. But that's not always the way it is.

How often does a parent come home from a miserable day at work and transmit his or her irritation and anger to the kids or their spouse? The attitude exuded is: "If it's been a bad day for me, it's gonna be bad for everybody!" Or those emblazoned sweatshirts that say, "If Mama [or Daddy] ain't happy, ain't nobody happy!" But that can never be the spirit of a disciple of Jesus. Because I am His disciple, He will insist on my loss of any right to require those around me to pay the price of my frustration—no matter how close to me they are! His way is clear: If you're going through a difficult, discouraging, hopeless day, be sure you take care of those near you. Don't transmit your trauma to them. They may share it with you (as Mary and John did with Jesus), but it shouldn't be dumped on them, nor should they be saddled with it involuntarily.

The best way to embrace hope is to understand the way that Jesus does it, and He is always more concerned with others than with Himself.

* * *

Has a personal tragedy caused you to lose hope? Praise is the pathway that will restore it. When anger, grief and broken-heartedness are met with faith-filled praise, our sorrow can be turned into joy and our fear into strength. Read Psalms 46–47.

CHAPTER 6

AIM YOUR HARD QUESTIONS AT GOD, NOT MAN

"My God, My God, why have You forsaken Me?"

MATTHEW 27:46

Here is the fourth way to find hope when you need it most: *Aim your hard questions at God, not man.* It is perhaps the most dramatic word spoken from Calvary. It trembles with pathos and emotional anguish, and nothing dramatizes it more passionately than the heart-piercing cry of God's Son, wracked with a sense of abandonment at the darkest moment of this very hopeless day: "Why? Why? Why have You left me now?"

The actual words Jesus cried out are quoted directly from Psalm 22, a song that by then was already a thousand years old—a lyric David prophesied before anyone could imagine God's Messiah would become the One to fulfill its agony. To glimpse but a part of it, read with me:

My God, my God, why have You forsak-
    en Me?
Why are you so far from helping Me,
And from the words of my groaning?
Oh My God, I cry in the daytime, but You
    do not hear;
And in the night season, and am not
    silent. . . .
All those who see Me ridicule Me . . .
[They say,] "He trusted in the Lord, let
    Him rescue Him;
Let Him deliver Him, since He delights
    in Him!"
But You are He who took Me out of the
    womb . . .
I was cast upon You from birth . . .
Be not far from Me,
For trouble is near;
For there is none to help.
Many bulls have surrounded Me; . . .
They gape at Me with their mouths,
Like a raging and roaring lion.
I am poured out like water,
And all My bones are out of joint;
My heart is like wax;
It has melted within Me.
My strength is dried up . . .
And My tongue clings to My jaws;

You have brought Me to the dust of death.
For dogs have surrounded Me;
The congregation of the wicked has
        enclosed Me.
They pierced My hands and My feet;
I can count all My bones.
They look and stare at Me . . .
But You, O Lord, do not be far from Me;
O My Strength, hasten to help Me!
        (vv. 1-2,7-19).

That was the cry of the psalmist in the spirit of the privileged candor God welcomes from those who worship Him. Tears are in His presence for He isn't the source of them; complaints are allowed for He alone can service their need. The counsel contained in Psalm 142 invites us to our call amid dark hours: "I cry out to the Lord with my voice . . . I pour out my complaint before Him" (vv. 1-2). Again, the message is clear: Aim your hard questions at God. You may not get the answer right then, but you can count on two things: (1) your cry never will fall on deaf ears, and (2) time will always bring an answer in your best interest. Always.

To scrutinize all the implications of this wrenching lamentation from the lips of Jesus seems beyond human comprehension. We might be able to imagine the breaking in His voice or the anguish of His heart, but who can fathom the mystery of the separation that was taking place or the depth of the pain it struck to the soul of God's Son? This outcry born of inner agony was not a performance for melodramatic affect. No! This was the Second Person of the Triune Godhead experiencing a breach in the fellowship He has known with the Eternal Father from before all worlds. And this separation—the cause of the forsakenness tearing at Jesus' mind—took place because Jesus ("[He] who knew no sin") was being made sin for us "that we might be made the righteousness of God in Him" (2 Cor. 5:21).

This concept staggers the finest theological minds and boggles the imagination of any who thoughtfully weigh its reality. And though the Bible explains it in the above words from 2 Corinthians, and though the psalmist prophesied it long before the Son became flesh to fulfill His saving mission in our behalf, I don't know that any human being can grasp the deepest mystery of the moment. But I do know two things are clear:

First, as the Son of God, Jesus is suffering in Himself the divine fulfillment of the ancient lesson taught in the Old Testament image of the scapegoat—the sin-bearer creature that was cast out from the camp, carrying all the guilt of the people. In His death, somehow Jesus is totally absorbing in Himself both the guilt and the penalty of *all the sin of all the ages*—a feat that can only be explained in that His qualifications as a *sinless* Savior provided space for *all sin* to be swallowed up in His own Person. Then, in dying, He fully broke the power of sin to ever again rule anyone who puts their life within the redeeming circle of His resurrected life!

Second, as the Son of man, Jesus is wrestling with an inexplicably dark depression, transcending description and beyond survival except for the miraculous sustaining power of the Holy Spirit. It is that grace alone, Hebrews 9:14 tells us, that enabled Him to complete the offering of Himself to God as sacrifice in our behalf. Yet notwithstanding His divinity and the divine strength accomplishing this eternal and cosmically encompassing feat, the Lamb of the Cross was fully human as well. And He was devastated by the vacuum void of the Father's presence—bitterly crying as He now actually drinks the cup He'd pled in Gethsemane to avoid.

This is the central moment of Calvary: It is the fourth of seven words. It is filled with questions, with darkness, with a sense of ultimate forsakenness—*God-forsaken!* Even if none of us ever experiences the dimension of Jesus' depression,

we have all had moments when we have wondered, "Why, God?" It's then we know that we
not only have a Savior who has been there and
understands our despair, but we have His example pointing us in the right direction. When
you're in the middle of a heartbreaking, hopeless
day—or worse, when you feel sure you've lost
touch with heaven and are mystified in your loneliness—aim your hard questions at God, not man.

Why? Because in life's darkest hours, there are
usually no human beings with adequate answers.
Counselors may analyze; associates may sympathize; experienced friends may empathize. But finite
minds and feeble flesh can never satisfy us with the
Presence we seek, for what we truly cry for is God
Himself, not "answers." When "bad day blues" turn
black with the unanswerable, and everything you
thought you knew backfires, forget human philoso-
phies or riddling theologies. Cry out to God. He
doesn't mind our complaints, and although He may
seem absent, He's never far away. Ask my friend Bill.

The deal had crashed. It involved a seven-digit,
high multi-million dollar figure for his corpora-
tion. After months of careful planning on the
human side, and after more than two years of
prayerfully seeking God's will and wisdom on the
divine side, Bill, as CEO, had led his company to

the brink of a pivotal acquisition. The funding was in place, and the promise of a broad range of new possibilities was open before them. All the company's stockholders had been advised of the impending purchase, and the press was watching expectantly because of the innovation manifest in the development. And best of all, Bill's own soul was clear before God as he moved forward with the plan.

Though the acquisition would advance profits dramatically, Bill knew his own heart before God. He had laid it before his Lord again and again during the many months before. He and his wife, Marie, had prayed together with unity and humility: "Dear Father, we want nothing but Your will for our company, exactly as we want it for our marriage. You are the Center of our lives: not success, not wealth, not recognition. We seek Your direction and blessing on Your terms, Lord. And whatever distills of profit or advancement we present to You in its entirety, not as a bribe to secure Your blessing, but as a sacrifice to honor Your Name."

Then somebody pulled the rug out. The whole world began disintegrating around Bill like a rocket exploding on a pad at Cape Kennedy, the gantry tipping wildly from its base, its framework shattered and falling apart.

The whole deal collapsed, and worse, the other company, which had entered the agreement in apparent good faith, had not only violated the carefully constructed terms, but had secretly conspired to make it look like Bill was the culprit. Compounding his frustration was the fact that the other company's CEO claimed to be a Christian and was in many respects viewed as a man of spiritual values as well as moral principle. But driven by his own fears and trapped in a newly surfaced but self-imposed difficulty, the other leader had turned the tables in a self-protective way that trashed the business agreement and proposed Bill as the cause of the problem. Now Bill was being named as the source of the deal's ruin. His wisdom as a leader was in question, and his integrity as a businessman was being thrown toward the scrap pile. However there was an "out."

The dishonesty of the other company—the calculated conspiracy that was besmirching Bill's good name—could be easily challenged in court. All Bill had to do was register his case and go public with charges that would vindicate him, even though the deal would be lost. At that point, the Holy Spirit met Bill in his dilemma: God's Word summoned him beyond human wisdom to trust beyond tragedy.

With the doubts of his shareholders hanging over him like an impending cloudburst, and his employees perplexed by negative reports on their otherwise-trusted leader, Bill cried out to God. He was tempted to bitterness, stabbed with pain, and torn by confusion: "God, I don't get it! You know my heart. You know how I've sought You at every point. Why is this happening to me, Lord? I don't care about the loss of a potential expansion; You know that! But why have You thrown me out to the dogs of injustice?"

His complaint over the devastation of having sought God for direction, having received clarity and peace to proceed, and then seeming to have been forsaken by the One he had sought foremost to please was laid before God's Throne. It was not a rebel's act of defiance but a child's cry of bewilderment. He bent over in prayer, doubled up with the physical torture of a soul driven to the edge. And one day during that season of his pained outcry before God's throne, God's Word resounded in his soul: "Do not take your brother to court. Do not defend yourself. Let Me be your Defender instead" (1 Cor. 6:1-7; Pss. 7:10; 59:16,17; 62:1-8).

Remembering the Savior's words in Psalm 22—the source of Jesus' own cry from the Cross, "My God, My God!"—Bill was helped to wrestle through to his decision. His choice: "The deal may die, and my reputation be buried, but I will not defend myself." All human counsel would argue otherwise, but Bill determined to make his point of complaint, inquiry and defense solely to God. The outcome of his decision is almost too successful to be believed where human doubt, fear and anger over injustice usually recommend reprisal and retribution. But after an extended season, when things looked like they would never change, during which Bill daily faced the need for keeping his commitment of trust to leave his case with God, a full resolution was realized. The deal was resurrected. No parties were embarrassed. All inequity was rectified. And Bill never openly revealed the details of the whole story—not even afterward.

There is a price to making God your point of reference when the hard questions raised in the middle of a hopeless day rack your mind and torture your soul. It's the price of listening to His answers and deciding whether or not to submit to His way rather than our own. Yet the rock-solid truth remains, the evidence of God's Word provides the unchanging, timeless assurance again and again: Your cry never will fall on deaf ears. And there will always be an answer—in His time—and that answer will be in your interest. Always.

* * *

Did an unexplainable event ever cause you to question God's promise to you, even just for a moment? Have you found it difficult to hang on to hope when you can't see what's ahead? Jesus assures us *He* is the Beginning and the End, and that "he who overcomes shall inherit all things" (Rev. 21:6-7). Read Hebrews 11.

CHAPTER 7

BE HUMAN ENOUGH TO ACKNOWLEDGE YOUR NEED

"I thirst!"

JOHN 19:28

Among the words Jesus spoke from the Cross, the fifth and sixth statements are uniquely linked. Although their content is radically different, the gospel record in John 19:28-30 makes it clear that Jesus asked for the drink of water for one primary reason. It wasn't the most obvious—simply slaking thirst—though the ordeal of crucifixion would be more than reason to cry out for a drink. The horrific energy drain, the perspiration amid trauma, the bloodletting—all would produce rapid dehydration. Furthermore, Jesus had earlier turned down the offer of a drink, including a pain-dulling prescription that not only might have satiated a degree of thirst, but would likely have reduced mental acuity (see Mark 15:23). Instead, the Lamb of Calvary chose to retain command of His senses; any escape from pain or other temporary comfort was not on His agenda.

The one reason Jesus asked for something to drink had to do with what He was about to say. The biblical setting made that unmistakably clear. As the Word incarnate was about to bring His final sermon—a message for all time, to first be proclaimed from the elevated pulpit of His Cross—He needed to clear His voice. The announcement to follow was not to be muttered or choked out but trumpeted so all mankind throughout all history would be able to hear it. But to prepare for that moment, He needed help.

Let me emphasize this carefully, for there is a very practical point for our discipling lessons here on this very hopeless, very bad day. Make no mistake, Jesus was dying, but He was also fully in control of this moment. Everything taking place was *His* choice. It was true that He could summon an angel host to deliver Him. It was true that no one could take His life, but He chose to lay it down.

And that point—His capacity to *choose* as He willed—is central to our seeing the next truth, so important for us all when we go through hopeless days. Here it is:

Jesus' plea for a drink of water is a reminder that no one is so in control, so spiritual, or so self-sufficient that they can make it through a hopeless or bad day without people to help them.

The lesson for us all is centered in *why* Jesus made known His need, not only that He did. His purpose, as we have noted, was that there would be clarity in the statement He was about to make, and there are parallels to our hopeless days as well.

A hopeless day can blur our perspective and muddy our speech. It can fog the mind and bring uncertainty to our hearts, or tempt us to mutter words of dubious wisdom unless we are willing to let our need be known to others. On a hopeless day, humbling yourself to ask the help of others can help you clarify the stance you're taking in trusting God. This is no prompting to seek the shallow refuge of someone to pamper you by mouthing self-pitying complaints. But just as the drink offered to Jesus, though bitter, still helped clarify the confession of faith He was about to bring, you and I need the encouragement we can bring to each other.

That was certainly what Anna and I discovered following that dismal day the phone rang with the pathology report following the biopsy of the polyp removed from her colon.

Few things seem to paralyze faith more readily than one word: *cancer*. Retaining hope often seems a form of denial before the monstrous facts of this beast's ongoing harvest of multitudes. Notwithstanding the efforts of dedicated researchers and the helpful advances made in battling this sinister opponent, when cancer touches your family, your world is suddenly clouded by a very bad day.

Neither of us will ever forget the long drive that afternoon after the phone call. The doctor was sensitive, kind and understanding. But he was also professional, direct and realistic. There were things that could be done: surgery to elect, post-surgical treatments to be determined, actions to take that offered no guarantees; only percentages of likely removal or remission could be quoted.

That hopeless day was a sunny, springtime afternoon, but the quiet beauty we had sought on our drive through the nearby mountains—to talk together with oft-quavering voices on the edge of tears before the worst of all prospects— was little comfort.

Though my left hand was always firm in its grip of the steering wheel, my right hand was in constant touch with Anna as we discussed all the possibilities. I held her hand—periodically caressing it tenderly, occasionally patting her knee assuringly. Sometimes I simply stroked her forearm, realizing the very physical frame I was touching, containing the dearest person to me on this earth, was also carrying a death sentence within it.

Our conversation was not fatalistic.

Anna and I have prayed for hundreds over the years, and we have seen many precious people healed, but we have also seen many die. Now, here we were needing more than our own prayers. Yes, we had excellent doctors caring for her, and we were certain their skills held the best possibilities. Yes, we also knew, above all, that her life—indeed, ours together—was in the hands of our loving Father. And yes, we have a loving family too; there was no question about their concern and support. But there was a question: How do we discuss this with the congregation?

There are certain difficulties wrapped in the high privilege of being entrusted with a very large church. Ten thousand members may sound impressive to the casual observer, but each one is simply another sheep in the pastures of the Great Shepherd. Irrespective of the number who call you "Pastor," serving them as one of His own sheep yourself, while serving Him as a sheep-become-shepherd to others, sometimes requires wisdom in deciding how much of your own burden you should share with them.

For us, it was not a question of feeling guard-ed against appearing "human." To the contrary,

ON A HOPELESS DAY,
HUMBLING YOURSELF TO
ASK THE HELP OF OTHERS
CAN HELP YOU CLARIFY THE
STANCE YOU'RE TAKING IN
TRUSTING GOD.

we have never hidden ourselves or pretended to be "above" any of the basic things that are common to our humanity. Nor did we feel obligated to demonstrate some great optimism or verify a stoutly religious affirmation of our absolute certainty we were expecting God to vindicate our faith or verify our ministry with a miracle. Rather, our question as to what degree we should share our problem with our flock was tied up in a mixture of feelings—of concerns such as (1) not wanting to exploit the emotions of the congregation in our interest when there are always so many others in the church who need love and support more than we do; (2) hoping to avoid discouraging those feeble sheep who, being young or weak in faith, become stultified or unduly set back in their view of God if someone they deem beyond problems faces a huge one; (3) wondering to what degree a public mention of Anna's disease would excite a rash of good-willed but misguided approaches by those wanting to "come and lay healing hands on her" or those offering advice on alternative remedies. We were not ill-disposed toward any means by which anyone would propose care, but we were uncertain as to how much traffic we could tolerate, however well intended, once word was given concerning her condition.

That day, we talked and prayed our way to the only conclusion we felt was consistent with both the Word and the Spirit of God, which have always been our best and ultimate point of reference. Over the next few days we met with key members of our staff, as well as the elders of our church, and spelled out the whole situation to them. Unsurprisingly, we received their loving support, which was joined to their confirmation of our decision.

The Sunday following this process—eight days after hearing the medical report—we presented ourselves to the whole congregation. The elders had prepared for the Communion of the Lord's Table to be served as we gathered in God's presence. I preceded any mention of Anna's condition with a brief teaching on the need of every member of Christ's Body toward the others (see Rom. 12:4,5; 1 Cor. 12:12-26). Then I related the facts pertaining to Anna's physical circumstance and spoke of our desire not to distract the congregation from larger issues by reason of their affectionate concern over ours.

In short, like Jesus on the Cross, we were acknowledging our "thirst." It was not for personal attention or for sincere, yet unsought, pity but for helping us to clearly live out—to enunciate through wisdom pragmatically applied in the face of a hard situation—a declaration of faith, hope and peace, whether by life or by death.

It was one of the most memorable days in the life of our congregation. There were tears, but they were not born of either fear or discouragement. There were Holy Spirit-prompted words of encouragement and confidence amid trial, but they were not born of either religious excitement or legalistic triumphalism. There was joy at the Lord's Table where we partook together in remembrance of Calvary's victory beyond apparent loss and where we also embraced the promise of hope for healing. Elders anointed Anna with oil in the name of the Lord Jesus Christ, and the congregation rose with high praises to God for His Word, which undergirds us in all life's trials and goes before us unto ultimate victory.

The results were manifest over the days, weeks, months and years to follow. First, the congregation stood firm with us throughout the ordeal of Anna's surgery and post-surgical season, but they didn't capitulate to doting preoccupation or emotional distraction. Gracious concern was always present, but overweening attentiveness was thankfully absent.

And Anna was healed!

No, it wasn't instantly. Yes, the surgeon's hands were involved. No, we didn't experience immediate release from fears. Yes, great prayer and faith were exercised and brought enormous hope beyond reason and peace beyond explanation. And without question, there were marked events within the flow of the whole ordeal that exceeded human wisdom or skill, and there were results that our doctor was free to acknowledge as manifesting a gracious providence. In it all, that Providence, our loving Lord, transcended the best that human care could accomplish and manifested His merciful hand in a complete recovery. Why? Not because of any worthiness on our part; certainly not without the partnership of an entire congregation who heard us say, "We need help in order to pursue our path with clarity and with faith."

Jesus' fifth word from Calvary calls us to learn this point of discipleship, especially when hopeless days come upon us. It is one thing to fortify ourselves and brace against the storms of life's bad days, but it is another to humbly acknowledge our need of each other. It's an inescapably important principle to apply: If the Son of God requested help during Calvary's struggle, I am wise to remember that I will have times I need to ask for help—for human assistance as an avenue of divine grace. It is neither immature nor self-pitying. It is the balance taught in the words of Galatians 6, which seems to contradict itself, saying, "Each one shall bear his own load" (v. 5), after declaring, "Bear one another's burdens, and so fulfill the law of Christ" (v. 2). But the distinctive words of the original text contrast our personal "responsibilities" (v. 5) with the "overload" that life sometimes deals every one of us.

It's the very model seen here in the Person of Jesus. He isn't seeking respite from responsibility; He needs help in the midst of physical overload. And when we look at the Savior crying, "I thirst!" we see yet another principle of hope for a hopeless day. In tough times, I need the help of others to enable and assist me to clarify my confession of my faith. Further, when hopelessness would dry my soul, I need hands to steady mine, assisting me to drink deeply of the cooling waters that drive the hell-fires of doubt and fear backward, and remove the smoke from my eyes so that, in God's grace, I can see the hope His tomorrows for me always hold.

* * *

Are you hesitant to be open and transparent with other people? Did anyone ever say to you, "Don't get your hopes up"? When we put our trust in Jesus Christ, we become members of His Body, joined together in His abundant life *today* and eternal hope forever. Read Ephesians 4.

CHAPTER 8

BE ASSURED, THERE IS A PURPOSE AND AN END

"It is finished."

JOHN 19:30

Tetelesthai—It is finished!

The most significant single word in the Greek New Testament translates to the most triumphant declaration. It contains both a prophecy and a verdict. Jesus, the Son, prophesies the momentarily impending conclusion of His saving work, and *even before the Cross's finale,* He anticipates the Father's verdict and His ultimate intervention.

The atoning sacrifice of the Lamb was accomplishing eternal salvation.

The deliverance of humankind was as possible as Israel's deliverance from Egypt more than a millennium before.

The dawn of world redemption had broken, and with it the chains of human slavery to sin, shame and condemnation were being shattered.

Though they were the most climactic, those were not the final words spoken by the Savior from the Cross. He will shortly commend His Spirit into the Father's hands. But He is already confident; His declaration of triumph is being registered. The grounds are now established at a dual dimension, welcoming fallen humans back into fellowship with the Father and driving back the powers of evil from their dark and damning rule over humankind.

The essence of the magnificence in these words is their finality as a statement of faith. The ultimatum they declare is absolute, even though the victory is not yet visible. "It is finished!" is the Son of God's own invitation to join Him in the conviction that *now—because of the Cross—there is nothing we struggle with that is without either a purpose or an end.*

No struggle need ever again be pointless.

No suffering need ever again be unending.

The Master not only announces salvation's total accomplishment, but near the climax of His difficult day, He summons us to embrace this truth when we're agonizing through ours. He is teaching us to learn and live in this light:

First, to know that we never face any assault of flesh, devil, circumstance or personal weakness without God's hand present, mighty and available to work through it all—and beyond it all. This doesn't mean God has planned every bad thing that happens to people. Evil things that are initiated by hell's hatefulness or by human sin, failure and rebellion create their own problems. But beyond them all, God's ultimate deliverance is our promised inheritance.

Second, Jesus' words, "It is finished!" are to lead us each to understand that even before our personal ordeals are over, we are privileged to invite God's sovereign presence and power to invade our hopeless days, releasing His triumphant grace to achieve His purposes in the end. The most incredible proposition in the universe is that the Sovereign of all creation awaits the invitation of frail humans. But once invited, the Father's transcendent power is ready to intervene—introducing a wisdom and might that is greater than anything producing the worst of our hopeless days.

The Cross demonstrates this point. When you're living through a difficult day, don't expect to be able to "read" the full dimensions of God's redemptive plan in the middle of your struggle, but never doubt the certainty that it is in process. His call, "It is finished!" is our call to hold firm in this assurance: His sovereign power will ultimately win the day.

Karl and Pamela's baby died. The ordeal had been in progress for months. A horrible tumorous intrusion was crowding into the tiny infant's cranium, and at daybreak that Sunday morning the phone rang at our house. I spoke brief words of sympathy to the family friend who had called, advising me that the baby had succumbed to death, and almost immediately, I left for the hospital. Karl and Pam were a strong pair in our congregation; they were parents already to three children, and they had so anticipated baby Jason's recovery, which would maintain a "two boys and two girls" evenness in the family.

I had wept with them the day before, bowing in prayer and uttering the one phrase the Lord had put on my lips: "Sustain this little boy *unto life*, O Lord, *unto life!*" I could not pray anything else, and I didn't give any interpretation to what I did pray. I have heard wonderful reports of miracles, especially in cases involving children, where God's creative reconstructive interventions have turned apparently futile circumstances into triumphant ones. We have had a small share in experiencing some of those miracles in our church family, but I have never felt it my privilege or assignment to declare one in advance of its occurring. Still, I had passionately prayed, *"Unto life! Unto life!"* But on the morning after, I was on my way to comfort a couple in a situation where death seemed to have won.

I turned the corner out of the subdivision where we lived, and I was slowing down to stop at the intersection's flashing red signal. It was still early, there was no other traffic, and as I slowed I noticed a small object in the roadway. As I drew up to the crosswalk (there were no cars behind to goad me on after my stop), I got out to see what it was, feeling strangely moved to do so. There is no way to explain either my prompting or the scene which I saw other than to attribute it to the Living God, Who works both signs as well as wonders. A dead sparrow lay there in the street—its head completely removed! The instant I saw it, a Voice deep within me—unprompted by human reason—whispered a message with clarity and conciseness: *"Not one of them falls to the ground apart from your Father's will . . . Do not fear therefore; you are of more value than many sparrows"* (Matt. 10:29,31).

Returning to the driver's seat, I resumed driving to the hospital, my eyes brimming with tears and my mind racing even while my spirit soared with a deep sense of heaven's purpose invading Karl and Pam's moment. Whatever anyone else might say, I knew I had seen a sign, for there was no explanation why the bird would be lying there headless unless some purpose of God had arranged it. If a cat had snatched the bird and taken its head, it would have consumed the whole body. If a car had run over the bird, the head would have been on the pavement. Whatever happened—and at a timing that coincided with my arrival at the intersection—a message was clearly spoken to me: *This baby whose head was taken is gone, but Father God wants you to be reminded that the child is precious to Him, and that he is of great value to the Father!*

That I felt this so profoundly was one thing. But how to relate it to a bereaved couple was another. It seemed to me that, notwithstanding anything within my own conviction, it could strike them as painfully contrived. But my uncertainty was instantly removed when I walked into the hospital room where Karl, Pam and the couple who called me were embracing one another—praising God and worshiping Him for His goodness! These were not religious freaks, nor were they glib fanatics who blithely philosophize tragedy with a happy smile and a trite quoting of something like, "Everything is okay if you believe it's true." These were honest-to-good-sense people who had been caught in the grip of God's grace and who had been persuaded by the Holy Spirit's comforting presence that beyond the tragedy, God was at work doing something grand. They didn't blame God or a deficiency of faith in Him for the event. They weren't bantering theological catchphrases or philosophical opinions. They had been secured in the arms of the Father and assured by the steadying pulse beat of His heart: *There is a purpose to unfold from Jason's short life, and there will be an end to your sorrow as well.*

Greeted with their warm embraces, I listened to their description of God's gentle preparation of their hearts for the baby's passing, and I prayed with praise alongside them. Then, sensing the presence of the Holy Spirit's having worked such a wonder in these two bereaved hearts, I ventured telling them of my experience while driving to the hospital. The response was, by now, predictable. No one needed to strain to make room for the episode, as though their spirituality was being tested by their response. They were stirred: "Indeed, Pastor Jack, the Lord is emphasizing the point. He has not only worked redemptively here in removing the pain of death's sting from our hearts in this moment, He is also confirming to us that there is a purpose in this, not just a tragedy."

"From Tragedy to Triumph" suddenly became the theme of the day. The moment was so visited by divine grace that I couldn't help risking a suggestion: "Karl, Pam, let me ask your permission on something. I don't want to do anything that would risk appearing to exploit the emotion of the moment, but may I ask if you would feel offended if I shared the story of this ordeal, along with this morning's events, with the congregation?" I could hardly believe my own ears. It was 6:45, and the first service would begin in 45 minutes. I had a message ready, but I felt God had another one for our church family that day. Karl and Pam agreed . . . and the rest, to adapt a phrase, "is all He wrote!"

God inscribed a holy memory into the life of an entire congregation that day. He answered the doubts of people who wonder about premature death. He neutralized the superstitions that cause people to feel obligated to say God "designs" this kind of human agony. He fit together a combination of biblical good sense with human understanding. The result was not only a swelling of praise to God for His triumphs amid apparent tragedies, but that morning, more than 35 people received Jesus Christ as their Savior! (Yes, I did tell the sparrow story, and yes, the Holy Spirit made it credible to all hearts present, not as a rationalization but as a gracious, illuminating providence, reminding us of God's very personal care for each of us.)

His personal care is the reason that the events of any of life's hopeless days are a potential staging ground for the wonder of His redemptive working. It's why, going through a difficult day, there is still a reason to declare, "It is finished." All His purposes are secured and will be fulfilled, and whatever the present suffering, there is an end.

Weeping may endure for a night, But joy comes in the morning (Ps. 30:5).

* * *

Are you willing to invite Jesus into your most hopeless day and to receive the provision He has for you? Though God does not design our hopeless days, His Son Jesus can redeem them to full glory. Read John 14.

CHAPTER 9

FINALLY, SURRENDER YOUR DAY TO GOD, AND LET IT GO!

"Into Your hands I commit My spirit."
LUKE 23:46

When you come to the end of any day that's been a hard day, it's usually as difficult to conclude as it has been to live. The end of the day can be the start of a long night of reliving the day's struggle and of missing the restorative powers of sleep through the restlessness of a night as bad as the day. So in seeking to lay hold of this last principle, letting Jesus disciple us to navigate beyond hopelessness to hope becomes all the more important.

This is especially true when you know the day you're ending might not be much different from tomorrow!

Hopeless "days" can be weeks long, and the constituted agenda may not be rapid in its passing. Some things never go away fast enough, and the soul—the heart, mind and emotions—can become preoccupied to the point that they wheel over and over with the same cycle of thoughts, the same pinching of pain, the same specter of fear or the same bewildering doubts—all of it attended by the relentless question, "When will all of this go away?"

To find hope when you need it most—indeed, to conclude that bad day—is to *place it into the hands of God and leave it there.* This is how the agony of Calvary came to its conclusion, and it is important to understand what these words *didn't* mean as well as what they did. On the lips of Jesus, "Into Your hands I commit my spirit" is no more an act of wearied resignation than "It is finished" was a cry of defeat. Both are assertions—statements of definitive action. The sixth "word" was one of *triumph*, the seventh one of *trust*.

Never let it pass your notice that the dying Lamb is also the Prince of life. The Sacrifice is also the Priest—Jesus Himself being, at once, the presented atonement and the presenting officiant. *His* was the life being laid down; *He* was the One laying down His life. And the hours of agony accomplished their purpose: The atoning blood was shed, and the grace of forgiveness was initiated on eternally worthy grounds, for salvation was all but paid for. The blood of the Lamb was shed, and all that remained was His final surrender of life itself.

Months before, Jesus had made a categorical statement on the subject: "I lay down My life that I may take it again. No one takes it from Me, but I lay it down of Myself" (John 10:17-18). Now that moment had come.

There is something preciously sublime about Jesus' final words from the Cross. Not only are they generally overlooked, but to overlook them is to miss their message for us as His disciples. From the human perspective, His words indicate a colossal act of trust in the Father. He was surrendering His control of life into the Father's hands, whereas an hour before, He was torn with the agony of abandonment, feeling the distance between Himself as the bearer of our sin and the pure holiness of the Father Who is incapable of countenancing sin. But now, with nothing more than His confidence in the Father's fidelity to His own Word, the Son says, *"I'm ready to release My hold on life, and I'm unafraid to do so because I am placing everything about Myself into Your hands."* His words of trust, surrendering everything into the strong hands of the Almighty God, are His concluding lesson to us about how to find hope for a hopeless day.

Trina sat in my office, the picture of composure. An attractive woman in her early forties and the wife of a successful physician, she was the essence of social grace and cultural sophistication. But there was nothing in her of the snobbishness or superiority that undermines the true dignity of a person with such regal bearing, because Trina was a deeply devoted servant of the Savior. She had come to Christ several years earlier, and her growth had been marked by a humility as surely as her background had cultivated in her that gentle dignity. But Trina's husband had never come to the Lord.

I had seen Walt in church a few times, and in fact had met him once. Two things were clear. First, he had the genuine respect and an almost reverent regard for his wife's faith. It wasn't the formal respect that polite society requires, but a manifest esteem for a dimension of life he recognized she possessed and which contributed something valuable to their home and marriage. But there was a second thing—the evidence of a subtle deception that suggested to an otherwise reasonable mind that somehow he didn't need the Savior Jesus. Or more honestly put, "If you ever open to Him, it will mean *genuine transformation*, and you don't want to stop being who you really are, do you?" It was in Walt's face—a fundamental dishonesty with himself—the inevitable result of a knowing soul being dishonest with God . . . and knowing that, too.

But this was another day—a day at least three years into Trina's walk with Christ, and she had asked to see me. She was direct and to the point. "Pastor Jack, I want to ask more for your prayer than for your counsel, and it relates to something I feel convinced I am to do. I know it will seem radical and, by any definition, I suppose it is. I don't want to seem to have taken leave of my senses, but I don't know anyone else I can tell—nor do I plan to tell anyone else, other than Lisa, my closest friend.

"You've met Walt, and you know what a fine man he is. You also know that he isn't a Christian, despite his open acknowledgment to me that he knows he should give his heart to the Lord. I think you know me well enough to know I am not the nagging religious-wife type, and by God's grace, I believe I have obeyed the Word of God in the way I have *lived* and *loved* like a wife should. Walt does acknowledge this, and he has regularly expressed his gratefulness for my continued care for and attentiveness to him."

I was ready for the point to be made—one all too frequently asserted today by Christian spouses who say, "I've done everything I can, and I'm tired of trying: I want to get a divorce from my unbelieving wife (husband)." But I was spun for a complete loop when Trina continued the explanation of her prayer request.

"Pastor," she lowered her eyes, with slight embarrassment, "I don't want to seem at all inappropriate to you, nor do I wish to make this any more awkward than it already is for me. The fact is, Walt is having an affair. I recently discovered this as the result of finding some medication he left on the cabinet—medicine for the treatment of venereal disease.

"When I confronted him about it, he admitted both to the affair and to his having contracted the disease from the woman."

"Presuming you and he have been pursuing your normal sexual relationship," I inquired, "what in the world did he say to you in the light of your finding this out—seeing he is now exposing you to the same disease?"

She responded, "He was a mix of shame and humiliation. He raised no argument for himself, apologized for the craziness of his behavior, and yet went on to say that as ashamed as he is he couldn't promise he wouldn't yield again to the same temptation."

"Then, I suppose your prayer request is that I begin urgent prayer that Walt take this signal of his foolishness to drive him to the Lord," I suggested.

She affirmed the desirability of such continued prayer but went on to say that the real request she had was for her own physical protection. "You see, Pastor Jack, I believe I have every right to walk away from Walt or to at least deny him bedroom rights until, first, he is cleared of the infection and, second, he has called it quits with the woman."

I nodded my agreement, but Trina wasn't finished. "But I also believe the Lord is calling me to demonstrate my love for Walt in a way that will make an inescapable statement about God's love for him. Pastor, *I believe I am to remain sexually available to him, even though it could be at the risk of my life.*" She further described having found a magazine with photos of naked males in pornographic interplay, and wondered if Walt might be dabbling in ways that could even lead to her being exposed to AIDS.

"I know it's radical, Pastor. And I hope you will understand that my compulsion is something I believe the Lord has prompted me with and not some desperate need on my part to either sustain sexual activity or to clutch for my husband's affection. I can survive without the physical relationship, and I don't have any doubt that Walt cares about me. The problem is, he is a horribly blinded soul, and my hope is that 'loving him as Jesus loves us,' that is, *'while we were yet sinners, Christ died for us,'* might shock him into reality with the awfulness of his being lost. He's a bound soul. But he's my husband,

and I want to do anything I can to help him come to Christ."

I was as moved as I have ever been by one person's sense of marital commitment. Nothing—let me repeat—*nothing* in the Bible required this kind of caring on Trina's part; indeed, she had a biblical license to walk away from Walt. And *nothing* in my experience with dedicated followers of Jesus had ever surfaced a greater will or more dramatic commitment to self-sacrificing love for someone needing Christ. The words that came to mind as I prayed for her safety as she moved forward in this commitment were, "Father, into Your hands we commit Trina's life." They were the only hands that could shield her and secure her tomorrows.

A year or so later, Walt left Trina. He chose a promiscuous and perverted life instead of Christ—and instead of the devotedly marvelous woman he had as his wife. And Trina? She was never infected, though she continued as her husband's lover and faithful wife until the day he announced he was leaving. She kept her life constant in Christ, and though I haven't seen her for years, she still has a strong relationship with her children and with her Savior.

I have never proposed Trina's "surrender" as a model to anyone, but it certainly strikes an opposite chord to the readiness with which many

THE SAME ONE WHO
DIED TO OFFER US
ABUNDANT LIFE IN OUR
TODAYS—AND ETERNAL
LIFE IN TOMORROW'S
FOREVER—ADDRESSED
HISTORY'S CONSUMMATE
HOPELESS DAY IN A WAY
THAT TEACHES US HOW
WE MIGHT FACE OURS.

Christian believers will walk away from their marriages today, saying they are "hopeless." And marriage isn't the only arena in which we are often called to maneuver through the hopeless and the bad. There are dozens of life issues that call us to follow Jesus' pathway for realizing hope in a hopeless day—issues that are seldom as quick to pass as we wish they would and that always call us to the Cross to hear the Savior's words again . . . and again.

In Philippians 3, the apostle Paul expressed a life-long goal to know Christ "in the power of His resurrection," a goal to experience the dynamism of that supernatural dimension of life Jesus called "abundant"—the life He came to bring to us all. But those words do not stand alone. They have a companion phrase which points the pathway to "knowing Christ" in abundant-life power, for the sentence ends, ". . . and the fellowship of His sufferings, being conformed to His death" (v. 10). The charted course is clear. It is and always has been called "the way of the Cross."

The Cross of Jesus Christ not only calls us to *Him*—Who alone is "the Way, the Truth and the Life"; Who alone holds the keys of eternal life; Who calls us to receive His forgiveness and power through our repentance for sin; and Who calls us to faith in Him as God's Son, the only Savior—but the Cross also calls us to *a life,* to the wisdom of God's ways in all our relationships and pursuits, and to the pattern of Jesus' model in the face of our deepest struggles and most difficult trials. The same One Who died to offer us abundant life in our todays—and eternal life in tomorrow's forever— addressed history's consummate hopeless day in a way that teaches us how we might face ours.

- Forgive anyone—no, *everyone*—who seems set on ruining your life.
- Though beset yourself, focus on encouraging others who are struggling and uncertain.
- Be sure you are sensitive and loving, certain to take care of those who are near you.
- When seemingly impossible questions come, aim them at God, not at man.
- Whatever your adequacy, never be above making known your own need for help.
- Embrace the certainty that God's "finishes" *always* have a purpose and an end.

And finally, when it is all said, one thing remains to be done:

- Surrender everything to God and let go.

Those are the things we can see when we keep "looking unto Jesus," and they're the things that will see you through—*and beyond*—ANY "hopeless day."

There's a wonder that will lift my soul however
        dark the day,
There's a glory that will burn away despair.
It's because there is a Man Who died, then rolled
        way the stone
That would block the light of hope—then meets
        me there.

For He's always present, always there, just one
        step past my fears,
And He's reaching now to you—what e'er your pain.
So lift up your eyes—look unto Him—He's
        walked your path before,
And He knows the way that leads to hope again.

Just as sure as death could not contain Him, thus
        that Easter morn
He exploded every power that seeks to kill.
Just as surely, naught of hopelessness can stop
        His meeting you,
And He'll stay until your hopes have been fulfilled—
        It's His plan to bless, and best, it's all God's will.

—JWH

* * *

Is there a place in your life—perhaps a wounded relationship or a detoured dream—that you have yet to let go of and surrender to God? *Trust Him with it today*. He cares personally and deeply for you and has planned your life with a future and a hope. Read Psalm 139.

CHAPTER 10

HOPE FOR TODAY . . . AND FOREVERMORE

Blessed be the God and Father of our Lord Jesus Christ, who according to His abundant mercy has begotten us again to a living hope through the resurrection of Jesus Christ from the dead.

1 PETER 1:3

There's one more thing.

Jesus didn't *stay* on the Cross.

On the Sunday after that terrifying, hopeless Friday—the one known as "Good" but that seemed so horribly bad—there came a morning.

A morning filled with hope.

A morning in which an angel stood at the open door of Jesus' empty tomb and proclaimed the most hope-filled words the world will ever hear: *"He is not here; for He is risen, as He said!"* (Matt. 28:6).

That reality is both the spark and the fuel that ignites *all lasting* hope! Our possibility of recovering hope when hopeless days start to steal it is rooted in the fact that Jesus died on the Cross to break the back of everything that gives ground to hopelessness—our sin or failure, our fleshly weaknesses, temptation's snares, satanic devices or death's specter. *But!!* (Yes, emphasize that—punctuate it well—and fix it like that in your mind, dear one!) *But Jesus rose from the dead—He's alive forevermore, and He has the keys that loose all the cords with which hopelessness will seek to bind you or entangle your soul. Jesus has the keys to release HOPE!*

That does not mean everything changes at that moment—it means restored expectation begins to lift our souls from the quicksand of despondency, and the candle of faith begins to drive back the darkness. It means you'll find the Holy Spirit as a "come-alongside partner"—settling your soul with peace, focusing your faith on Jesus and undergirding you with everlasting arms until the time the full fruition of the Father's grace fulfills the resolution of matters that would otherwise destroy you.

This is exactly what Ephesians 1:15-23 describes in a prayer that cries out for you and me to have our heart's eyes opened—enlightened by the glory of God's victory in Jesus' resurrection and triumph over every adversary. That our vision be restored to see *"what is the hope of His calling and the riches of the glory of His inheritance in the saints."*

Those are the grounds on which we can stand; they are solid turf to sustain us. Measure their dimensions by allowing me to summarize them:

1. Jesus died to break the power of sin, death and hell.

2. Jesus rose again to demonstrate that hope has a living power to drive it unto the fulfillment of God's promises to us.

3. That life-giving, defeat-destroying, Satan-crippling, fear-smashing, doubt-dissolving power immediately sets in motion the outworking of God's great and gracious workings in our behalf.

4. And in the midst of any hopeless day, the Holy Spirit comes alongside us to support and encourage us, to comfort and assure us, and to lead and direct us as we abide in hope.

Review those, remembering that according to God's Word, "hope will never leave you embarrassed, but will see you through your tribulations and trials, all the while attended by the outpouring of God's loving Holy Spirit keeping you and deepening you through the experience of that process" (Rom. 5:3-5, JWH paraphrase).

Those "grounds" were the granite, rock-like base that I described myself standing on that dark morning that I related to you at the beginning of this book. Having walked together with you through these pages, I want to conclude by sharing a very personal experience that is intended to illustrate how the Lord wants us to understand how *real* the promised presence of His Holy Spirit is when we face tough times.

In chapter one, I described how my beloved son, Scott Bauer, had collapsed, struck down by a ruptured aneurysm on the brain, and how that Friday morning, only hours later, I had been so bitterly assailed by the Arch-prince of Hopelessness—Satan, the adversary of your soul and mine.

Let me add a simple ending to the story of that morning. About 15 minutes after I rose from bed, I stood in the dynamic of that gargantuan inner strength that God's peace had granted as I awoke that second time. I put on my bathrobe and slippers and stepped outside as I often do to pick up the newspaper and to pray.

It was a beautiful time of the day, just as the sun was coming up over a towering ridge of maple trees that line our street. Those trees, flush with their brilliant, colorful display of gold and red autumn foliage, were evocative of God's precious words to me: *"I will give you the blessings of autumn."*

I felt a miraculously granted sense of being rested and strengthened, flooded over with, circled by and upheld within the peace of God that surpasses all understanding. I had put everything into the hands of Jesus, and this otherwise dark day had turned to a sunrise display of hope—hope beyond reason, a living hope beyond a dying son. What happened next is wonderful to relate but difficult to describe.

I would give in to the temptation to resist sharing what follows, for a well-reasoned hesitation presents itself: Simply put, I don't want to be seen as superstitious or thought of as a gullible soul. I'm not. But the fact is, when you or I seek God with readiness, He often responds in such personally suited and preciously appointed ways that we are hard put to know how to describe them to others.

It reminds me of reading Sheldon Vanauken's dilemma, which he shared with C. S. Lewis, describing Vanauken's feeling that God had arranged a specific appearance of a rainbow to comfort him as he drove home from the hospital where he had spent the last moments of his wife's life beside her. In a letter to the great Oxford-Cambridge don,

JESUS ROSE FROM THE DEAD—HE'S ALIVE FOREVERMORE, AND HE HAS THE KEYS THAT LOOSE ALL THE CORDS WITH WHICH HOPELESSNESS WILL SEEK TO BIND YOU OR ENTANGLE YOUR SOUL.

Vanauken inquired if Lewis would consider him
unsound in his thinking to suppose this providence was truly a display that had been somehow
timed and arranged by God in his interest.
Vanauken described how it had inspired encouragement and hope when he saw it. Briefly summa-
rizing the response and counsel written back to the
bereaved man, C. S. Lewis, one of the truly towering
intellects of the twentieth century, supported the
soundness of a reasoning that God's heart, will
and power are not only able to engage such a personal demonstration (while doing other things at
the same time), but that it is wholly rejoicing to
Him that we believe when these tender mercies are
shown us. (See *A Severe Mercy*, S. Vanauken, Harper
& Row, San Francisco, 1977.) So now, being for-
tified by that recollection, let me conclude both
my story and these pages I have written in a quest
to encourage your hope when facing hopeless days.

Shortly after rising, as I described above, I had
now stepped outside our front door and, while
walking across the front yard where the newspaper had been thrown by our delivery boy, a fleet-
ing thought brought a smile to my mind.

  Over the quarter-century we have lived in this
house, there have been early mornings when I have
stood there in the front of our home and been at

prayer in the stillness of the hour and, on a few occasions, an interesting "happenstance" has occurred: One or more doves would glide to our rooftop or to a highpoint in one of our trees, clearly taking their elevated perch to catch the warmth of the early sunlight. This had happened innumerable times.

But there were special times—only a few, but nonetheless, marked and memorable occasions through the years—in which the doves' appearance had impressed me as "being arranged" as a sign to lend a gentle confirmation of the Holy Spirit's attendance to my prayers (since there is record of God's Spirit being represented by a dove on occasion). I wasn't dependent upon those moments to secure my faith, nor did I seek them as a practice. But neither had I been disinclined to reject the sense of "special care" that attended my soul on the few occasions such had happened. (And, as an aside, I repeat, there have been hundreds of times a dove or doves alighted when I sensed no feeling of any special providence, nor felt desirous of conjuring one.)

But this very challenging morning, as I stooped over to pick up the paper, I will never forget whispering with a smile in my heart, "Lord, Your peace is so wonderful just now—but it would be nice to 'have a dove' this morning." Then, as I stood up, I turned to look at the tree and our housetop. There were no doves present . . . then, smiling again (mostly at myself), I said with a slight chuckle, "Jesus, even if a dove isn't there, I know You are, and I thank You for the peace that You've given me."

And at that moment—amazing, peculiar, and still to this very day stunning to my soul—a phenomenon occurred.

Instantly, there came a distinct and unexplainable movement of wind across the trees in front of our house—a breeze that was as inexplicable, naturally speaking, as it was beautiful in its display. With a smooth, continual "whoosh," the leaves were softly folded back, and an indescribable display of sunlight—like diamonds—sparkled through the trees in our yard. Amid the utter beauty of the moment and its absolute and distinct unlikelihood as an occurrence, I was dumbstruck with wonder. Then, a clear, gentle Voice spoke within my heart:

"There are other ways than a dove by which I reveal My Presence."

It was so real, so tenderly gracious and so significantly timed—my heart leaped within me, and I stood in the morning sunlight, arms upraised, and began to sing:

"He is our Peace, who has broken down every wall!

He is our Peace—He is our Peace!"

A worship chorus I had not sung for years sprang to mind, and I continued singing it—overwhelmed by the loving kindness and personally attentive ways of our Father:

"Cast all your care on Him, for He careth for you, He is our Peace, He is our Peace," and the song continued, quoting from the promise of God's eternal Word in the Spirit's inspired words given through the apostle Peter centuries ago: *"God resists the proud, but gives grace to the humble. Therefore, humble yourselves under the mighty hand of God that He may exalt you in due time, casting all your care on Him, for He cares for you"* (1 Pet. 5:5b-7).

So it was. And so I relate it—cautiously, yet boldly in another regard.

Cautious, because I in no way want to suggest it is our or my right to demand signs from God, while being bold to affirm that there are times His sovereign choice is to do so.

Cautious, because I would want no precious soul to ever feel less loved if no personal sign occurs on your "day." Yet I want to be very, very bold to announce that an Ultimate Sign has been given to us all: *Jesus is alive!* And the same power that was manifest in raising Him from the dead is present where you are right now—present to lift you from anything of hopelessness into the hope-filled-ness of His presence!

Look unto Him, dear child of God!

Just as we have learned from His dealing through His Cross, now lift your eyes to His Throne on high, where our resurrected, ascended Savior welcomes you to learn through His resurrection!!

Every hopeless day is only a Friday, and "Fridays" pass away. And while they may lead through a Saturday of waiting, even mourning, Saturday isn't the end of God's week, but the doorway to Sunday. And *every* one of them is a fresh reminder, "Because He lives, I can face tomorrow!"

That's more than poetry—it's a prophecy about any day that circumstance tries to name "Hopeless." It announces, "In Jesus' Name, the Savior to Whom I lift my eyes and look with praise— my faith made bold in the victory of His Cross, and my hope anchored in the glory of His triumphant resurrection—I'm renaming today:

"I'm calling it *Hope-filled*!"

A PRAYER FOR RECEIVING CHRIST AS LORD AND SAVIOR

Possibly you have read this entire book and yet somehow never come to a place of assurance of a personal relationship with God. If that is the case, this small addendum contains a prayer—and an offer at the end of it.

The prayer is to help you be direct and to pray according to God's promise of salvation in His Word and through His Son Jesus Christ. So if you have never invited Him into your life, if you've never personally asked Him to be your Savior, He is ready to hear you—right now.

Please permit me to welcome Him into your heart—into your own life. Simply bow where you are—even kneel, if you can and if you are in a place you can do that. Permit me, please, to help you pray—right now.

I'll pray a simple prayer first, then after that, I've written added words for you to pray yourself.

My Prayer

*Father God, I have the privilege of joining with
this child of Yours who is reading this book right
now. I want to thank You for the openness of
heart being shown toward You and I want to
praise You for Your promise, that when we call
to You, You will answer.*

*I know that genuine sincerity is present in
this heart, which is ready to speak this prayer,
and so we come to You in the Name and through
the Cross of Your Son, the Lord Jesus. Thank
You for hearing.*

(And now, you go ahead and speak your
prayer . . . He's listening.)

Your Prayer

*Dear God, I am doing this because I believe in
Your love for me, and I want to ask You to come
to me as I come to You. Please help me now.*

*First, I thank You for sending Your Son,
Jesus, to Earth to live and to die for me on the
Cross. I thank You for the gift of forgiveness of
sin that You offer me now, and I pray for that
forgiveness.*

*Forgive me and cleanse my life in Your
sight, through the blood of Jesus Christ. I am*

sorry for anything and everything I have ever done that is unworthy in Your sight. Please take away all guilt and shame, as I accept the fact that Jesus died to pay for all my sins and that through Him, I am now given forgiveness on this Earth and eternal life in Heaven.

I ask You, Lord Jesus, please come into my life now. Because You rose from the dead, I know You're alive and I want You to live with me— now and forever.

I am turning my life over to You and from my way to Yours. I invite Your Holy Spirit to fill me and lead me forward in a life that will please the heavenly Father.

Thank You for hearing me. From this day forward, I commit myself to Jesus Christ, the Son of God. In His Name, Amen.

An Offer

Above, before you prayed, I said I would make an offer—and it's freely available to you with no obligation other than the request that you use it. "It" is a small book I have written, *Newborn*. It's a simple guide to taking your early steps of faith in Jesus Christ with wisdom—and to learning the pathway to growth in Him. It's important to recognize the Bible's instruction, "As a newborn babe, receive the milk of God's Word so you can grow by it" (1 Pet. 2:2).

Newborn not only provides guiding principles for beginning in Christ, it also contains the Gospel of John—one whole book of the Bible. This book is a means of "getting underway," so please let me send it to you.

You can obtain *Newborn* by writing to "Newborn," Jack Hayford Ministries, 14800 Sherman Way, Van Nuys, CA, 91405. Be sure to mention in your letter that you are responding to my offer in this book. You may also contact our ministry by an e-mail to editor@jackhayford.com.

After you have received Jesus Christ as your Savior, I strongly encourage you to find a church that worships Him, honors God's Word and is led by trustworthy pastors. Ask to be baptized in water as Jesus commanded, and when you do, expect Him to fulfill His promise to fill you with the Holy Spirit's power for your life and growth in the will of God. Further help on these themes is available in resources on our website (www.jack hayford.org), but you will best grow in them by becoming part of a healthy, local congregation's family life and worshiping with others who love the Savior.

A PRAYER FOR INVITING THE LORD TO FILL YOU WITH THE HOLY SPIRIT

Dear Lord Jesus,

I thank You and praise You for Your great love and faithfulness to me.

My heart is filled with joy whenever I think of the great gift of salvation You have so freely given to me.

And I humbly glorify You, Lord Jesus, for You have forgiven me all my sins and brought me to the Father.

Now I come in obedience to Your call.

I want to receive the fullness of the Holy Spirit.

I do not come because I am worthy myself, but because You have invited me to come.

Because You have washed me from my sins, I thank You that You have made the vessel of my life a worthy one to be filled with the Holy Spirit of God.

I want to be overflowed with Your life, Your love and Your power, Lord Jesus.

I want to show forth Your grace, Your words,
Your goodness and Your gifts to everyone I can.

And so with simple, childlike faith, I ask You,
Lord, to fill me with the Holy Spirit. I open all of
myself to You to receive all of Yourself in me.

I love You, Lord, and I lift my voice in praise
to You.

I welcome Your might and Your miracles
to be manifested in me for Your glory and unto
Your praise.

I'm not asking you to say "amen" at the end of
this prayer, because after inviting Jesus to fill you,
it is good to begin to praise Him in faith. Praise
and worship Jesus, simply allowing the Holy
Spirit to help you do so. He will manifest Himself
in a Christ-glorifying way, and you can ask Him to
enrich this moment by causing you to know the
presence and power of the Lord Jesus. Don't hesi-
tate to expect the same things in your experience
as occurred to people in the Bible. The spirit of
praise is an appropriate way to express that expectation; and to make Jesus your focus, worship as
you praise. Glorify Him and leave the rest to the
Holy Spirit.

RESOURCES
BY JACK HAYFORD

Available at www.jackhayford.org
or by calling toll-free (800) 776-8180

The Parable of the Pennies (CD, Cassette, DVD)
>   Discover how tenderly God loves each and
>   every one, and how none are too far, too
>   unworthy, too fallen or too ruined by failure
>   to ever be forsaken by or beyond His reach.

31 Days Meditating on the Majesty of Jesus (Book)
>   Learn the character of Jesus by studying var-
>   ious names and poetic terms used to
>   describe the wonderful depth and scope of
>   His Person and ways. These 31 daily read-
>   ings on the Names of Jesus found through-
>   out Scripture will lead you through a month
>   of being strengthened through "thinking
>   on the Name of the Lord."

The Divine Visitor (Book)
>   Access growth and understanding of God's
>   love and grace for your life as you learn the
>   beauty of Jesus' coming to us, living among

us, being wounded and suffering for us, and bleeding and dying for us. He came to "visit us" in our own world of need, and this book helps explain how personal it all is.

Joshua–Possessing the Promise (DVD)
Experience Israel's journey toward the Promised Land in this set of video teachings in which Pastor Hayford brings spiritual encouragement aimed at helping anyone find and realize God's purpose for their life.

Three Keys to Releasing Life (CD, Cassette, DVD)
Gain a grasp of the keys that liberate life in these three messages on the power of forgiveness, praise and giving.

The King's College and Seminary, two accredited schools founded by Dr. Jack Hayford, is committed to building spiritually vibrant, biblically strong, theologically balanced, Spirit-empowered, ministry-equipped men and women. Classes are offered both on-ground and on-line. To begin, we highly recommend the course Christian Disciplines, developed by C. Fred Cassity, J.D., using Pastor Hayford's books *My Daily Walk* and *Living the Spirit-Formed Life.* For information or to register, visit www.kingscollege.edu or www.kingsseminary.edu, or call toll-free (888) 779-8040.

Also Available from Jack Hayford

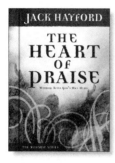